Wreath for the Red Admiral

Wreath for the Red Admiral

Patricia Clark

Spruce Alley Press
2016

Wreath for the Red Admiral by Patricia Clark

Copyright © 2016 by Patricia Clark

ISBN: 978-1-365-12064-0

Published by Spruce Alley Press, West Chester, Pennsylvania
www.sprucealley.com

First Edition: 2016
Set in Adobe Caslon Pro

Cover art, "Red Admiral," oil on canvas, by Stanley Krohmer

CONTENTS

"Coming east we left the animals
pelican beaver osprey muskrat and snake
their hair and skin and feathers
their eyes in the dark: red and green.
Your finger drawing my mouth."

from "The River Wolf," Jean Valentine

Wreath for the Red Admiral

A ragged morning with a tattered wing
like the red admiral yesterday's breeze
           carried into the back garden

up from the ravine, up from a sheltered spot
it had found in sunlight where it was contemplating
           warmth by basking in it.

The season two weeks ahead of itself, farmers
worried about the cherry crop—in orchards, they speak
           like painters, "pink too early."

How we waited all winter for sun, warmth,
to return, as hungry for it as we were for meat,
           for bread, for each other—

Common here, not migrating as far as the monarch,
the red admiral emerges any time of year—
           from a tree-high burrow hole, borrowed,

or from an inch thick space under cottonwood bark.
Admire its black wings edged with red-orange bands—
           white scallops on the tips.

I want to learn, living, how to be ragged on the wing
before another, loving the sun in each fiber and cell, not
           hiding where it's torn.

Air Like a Sea

I noticed the willow's long fronds
        hung down crimped
            like ringlets
      just unwrapped—
                and some birdsong,

notably the robin's, at midday
        came out ragged,
           a bit rusty
      and not so liquid—
                new leaves bore a fuzz

like the newborn's fontanel,
        without the throb
           though everything
on the wing seemed to be alighting,
              building, catching up

a catkin in its beak or scouting
        for worms or grubs.
           I wanted to place a finger
on the day's pulse,
              making it pause—

my fingernails like shells,
        the day's air a sea rolling in,
filling space around me,
        raising the beached kelp
                to sway alive, like hair

Winter Nests

(for Jane Leonard)

Study their look aloft, leaf-piles, stick and twig
laid down as lattice for a base, then stem upon stem
of leaves fastened and layered in together, not glue,
staple, or tape but interlock of twig and leaves,
edge and notch, heaped at a stout limb-snag, some
cracked, molded, bent, some interlain with fluff,
down of breast feather or blossom, frayed catkins a bird
tugged inch by inch from the yard waste heaped
out back behind the shed where a pile mounds up,
useful to robin, crow, or red tailed hawk, not spring
dwellings for hatching eggs, warming them, raising
a clutch but dark splotches, large, in a blasted
bare oak for a storm shield, a blizzard house when
it's this arctic, frigid—half dead landscape seared below.

Ecclesiastical

It is only that wild turkeys, single file,
make a dark processional through deep snow.

It is not that they represent anything.
They go searching for a thing to eat, scratching.

It is something to observe. No harm comes
to them—coyote or red tailed hawk.

But the woman who watches notes their slog
from east to west, how a subgroup tried

deviation, following the creek, and the one
in charge flew at them. Safety where

they circle, peck and bob for seeds, then flap up
heavily, ungracefully, to roost in bare

trees. This goes on day following day,
and she notes that soon the mating will start,

males parading their full display of gifts
as they strut, preen, turn like the Pope in sun.

The Prodigal Daughter

Now comes rainy May, gray skies, tulips laden with weeping.
Saw a weasel step across the grass.
First, there was a bronze hummingbird,
                        then the weasel turning its head.

In the tidepools, blood star with its thin arms
                        and red California sea cucumber.

No music after ten p.m.
Sparrows silent except for rustling in the hemlock,
                        whisper and wink of salmonberry.

Ghosts That Need Consoling

There's a black smear, low on the door-glass,
as though something tried to enter here overnight,
this place of books and a desk, my workplace.

Not a paw print exactly but an oily three inch smudge
with particles visible—stomach contents or shit
the only two options, I think. Five panes

in the door, narrow, from top of the door
to its base, where I step in from blue schist,
a wedge shaped slab that comes to an arrow point.

I'm the arrow, riding the red horse, tail out,
and me without saddle, bridle, reins—
arms out, too, like a warrior on the fly.

If there are bears nearby, as I believe,
maybe there's a way to learn their lore, a path
through dark woods by scent, feel, or a star.

There's an orange leaf down below on green—
glowing like a starfish on a piling in the sea.
I'm going there, no one can stop me—lost,

I'll find a bear or steer my way by dead
reckoning. Something needs settling, clearing
up, consoling—I told you something wailed

in the woods at night. It's what wants in.

By Clear and Clear: Riverside, Mid-Day

The old self dying away, you can feel it, can hear
a skeletal crack, then snap, as a ridgeline
breaks all down the thorax, the bony carapace
splitting, a faint odor lifting off, burnt hair
and a wet sizzle, the new lying there almost fetid
with freshness, with its own moist softness—
fetal, or maybe just larval, tender, exposed.
On all sides water, this again, the spit of land
liminal, pelagic, far from dry, your very steps
leaving an imprint in grass. Tomorrow you could return,
matching your prints to the day before—this day—
a child's game. Is that where the fractures go?
Now you walk emancipated, on the loose—out of the house,
its stale air, parents gone at last—grown-up, free.

Occurrence with an Elephant Head

When an elephant head comes into the room,
the scene is altered, the atmosphere of the atelier
shifts like tectonic plates slipping, wooden easels set on
crossbars start crying out to be adjusted, the painters' backbones

aching, primary colors daubed in rows onto glass
palettes grow prismatically brighter, the north light hues
waver greenly, all because an elephant head which is a skull
and lies first in a box, then is lifted out, raised on a platform

so many can view it, has a way of reordering thoughts—
now the room grows warmer, there is a whisper of savannah grass,
the far-off call of a cheetah pierces air, those in the room
knowing the sound without ever hearing it before, and there begins

a low rumbling, sub-sonic, not humanly heard but yet sensed,
toe-talking rippling out, tidal, an alarm quaking through the floor.

After Franz Marc's 'The Red Deer' (1912)

The apocalyptic future the artist saw long ago
shudders behind headlines in summer 2010—

red deer, necks snaking up to heads
sculpted finely, black noses and coal dark eyes—

white throats, bellies blushed with a smudge
bluish gray, otherwise downy and pale.

And the river's bloodied where they stand—
what will they drink?—They cannot sip fiery

rouged water, wading there, eating the palms
or Solomon's seal bending along the bank—

I grow frightened by the pale looming ghosts,
eyeless, icy cold, in the background—

my nightmare lurks there, dead, denuded world
that we created with our waste, our greed.

Ravine Goddess, August

She crooned, low, above the fetid smell
left by skunk overnight, then the notes
smoothed out, creamy, any ragged edges
disappearing, dissolved by rhythm, sound,
creek riffles moving downstream—though hurt
could still be heard, angling in the way a burr
catches by one prong, hanging on to fabric of shirt
or jeans—not easy to pry off, you'll try to shake
it without any luck. In the dog's hair, it works up
to a snarl, rat's nest, tangle you will have to
cut out with scissors. And always the most tender
of places—notch behind the ear, foreleg, rump
or belly hair close to the animal's sex. So try
the muzzle method—nip it out, lave with a wet tongue.

Heron, in Sunlight

It glittered, bent its neck,
      rummaged in its breast feathers
  for a speck of dirt, a flea,

and along I came with the dog,
      walking, watching as we do—
  most ordinary of all mornings—

That's it, my dear. No sweet
      promise of rescue, transport
  out of time—let's say

we were stuck in time, pinned—
      triad of self, dog, bird—
  before the moment went whirling

away, a flock of goldfinches
      wrinkled by, all scatter, burble,
  unstraight line, snippet of song.

Aerodynamic

Possibly sugar maple—
      this whirligig, samara, seed bearing
              bundle that sends
        DNA from the tree
out in the world to grow again.

Green loaded weight-
          bearing on one end, split to show
     an escape's in progress.

Its other end's a wing, flat
      bottom, curved top,
          in shades of tan, an edge
chartreuse or lime, depending on the light.

How one flies, descends, like
         a fallen leaf, an object beautifully lean.
     When today's walk brings you
out past the tall prairie grass,

and bedstraw, bloodroot—where hardwoods
send a trill of notes liquid
as rain from a singer hidden, you wonder,
can it be warbler, oriole?

        You must listen beyond
    yourself, become part sylvan, verdant,
breathing, swaying, there.

Tent Caterpillars

Terrible to look at them closely
through gauzy webbing,
how they writhe and twist,
a jumbled mass, squirming,
faceless, mouthparts moving, chewing—
are they eating the excretions
from others in their nest?

Sometimes men seize on a gem,
an idea of burning them out
with a gas-soaked rag held aloft
like a torch on a long pole—
the whoosh as the rag lights, an awful
purse-shaped bag of flame
blackening as the insects
ignite, consumed.

Kill the infestation but not
to light the shed—its wood
so crackling dry it wouldn't take
much, the sun's rays concentrated
on a nailhead heating up, spontaneously
combusting the nearby slats,
crumbling brown boards.

And the woods themselves, not to
stumble, toe caught on Virginia creeper,
ankle turned on a leafpile or log,
not to drop the pole, or let this
caterpillar nest-fire drop straight down,

liquid melt setting duff, mounded oak leaves,
deadfalls, last year's Christmas tree ablaze—

and if you do—the quickness with which
it catches, runs, blows up to the treetops—
lighting them. How many nightmares
of fiery extinction, this purge to destroy
a spreading pest but rescue the cottonwood?
How many visions of a thing burned clean,
the mass destroyed, what's left made
beautiful by riddance, a scouring flame?

Oscine

Singing tribes, from hidden perches, from stems
          and blossoms—honeysuckle, trumpetvine,
     clematis—from a cottonwood's high branch
  or the top spire of the white pine,
           this warbling, crooning, cooing.

Seldom from the ground, from a low place—why
        is that? Some fasthold with security,
    safety, a haven—or something about shade, semi-
  dark, coolness, looking out
          and then to lift one's voice, here.

From the ecotone, edges, margins, trees into field,
        lawn into hem of the woods,
    riverine bank, creek, tree limb,
  from the tree's dark trunk, rain-slick,
          from the leaf's umbrella-shade—

Song to braid this new day or darkening gloom,
        notes to send out, testing what the voice
    can do—trills, legato, runs and rasps,
  rattle of tongue against palate, mix of ecstasy,
          elegy, sound into art.

Rockweed, Knotted Wrack, Dead Man's Fingers

This is the rocky intertidal—stones,
    boulders, slabs tumbled together,
  thrown up here, left jagged by storms
     that batter land,
   and these the plants and algae
 wedged into crevices, cracks, sheer rockface.

Three levels of tidepools like stepping into caves,
    caverns of the mind as you go down—
  our guide warns that dark means
     most slippery—take care and crouch
   low to the ground, make a handhold
 of seaweed, surprisingly strong
      where it adheres.

Now sea anemone, amphipods, tortoiseshell limpets—
    tough attachers, limpets make their move
  at high tide, after, moving over rock
     to clean off, take in,
  what algae has stuck to stone, a banquet
   with a tang of sea salt, Atlantic air.

Discarded at the high tide line before descent—
    baggage of notebook, pen, field guide,
  lotions and spray to ward off bugs,
     the sun. Why so often
   at the shore, seaside, the margin, the brief
 deep, intimate talk? I barely know
      these people of half a day.

Carl mentions, first, the friends they partied with
            of a summer night, how two days later,
    after the stroke, the woman lay blind,
                without speech or movement—
    Beth, leaning close to him, laughs
            at her own mortality, says prednisone, shunt.

Turning over a rock or two, a hand thrust in
            to the wrist—dog whelk, red nose clam,
    hermit crab lugging its spiral shell-home
            and green crab, rock crab,
    barnacle. The tidepool tales are ones
            of adapting, small and large changes—
                some sudden, slow, fixed—

to adverse circumstances—the weather, tides,
            temperature going up or down, variation in food
    source or amount. Knotted wrack over time evolving
            float bladders from its own membrane
    to keep foliage lifted up—seeking life-
                giving light.

Of this hour only, we find ease against coastal boulders,
            themselves soaking up sun.
    Why go back now, step inside?
                No other life than this—
    the raw sea air, pungent pools of scrabbling life
            and death—everywhere you look scraps of claw,
                exoskeleton, bleached, abandoned.

Homage to the Green Heron

To the heron
standing near the bridge span
so quietly
and obscurely
like a pillar
or a stalk of teasel—
who would notice
or care
in this light?

And yet I spied
a glimmer of green
iridescent in crepuscular
light, slowing
my step, coming to
a quiet halt
with the dog, she
who sat then
at my feet.

The moment went on
lasting, the gray
almost tangible light
dimming further,
the heron not blinking
or lifting a wing
but holding in a posture
of deep thought,
perhaps, or sleep—
was that it?
No, the heron's eyes—

yellow-rimmed, opened—
and it turned its slender
beak back and forth,
neck hunching down
more into its shoulders,
a conductor
of air.

Heron, I admire
your subtle greenness
and even more
the stillness with which
you approach the coming
dark. How easy
you make it seem
to live in the world,
to stand, one-footed,
by a rusted bridge,
ignoring the querulous mallards,
never silent, never alone,
paired, forever paddling.

How can I say
I know anything
about the green-backed heron
without seeing it open
its glorious flexible
wings, flying off low
and thoughtful, to its
creekside nest?

Yet the call
to keep moving comes—
the dog shaking the leash—
and from the heron
I sensed a thought crossing
to me, mind to mind,
urging me to step on.
Not for today the chance
of seeing the heron drop
a bug on the water's surface,
using a twig or an insect
to lure some hungry fish
to the water's mirrored top.
To save a treat for another
day, to breathe where
your feathers are—
and there we went, swinging
along into sharp air, the river
lifting its voice with the wind.

Bird Carrying a Cranberry Necklace

(after Wallace Stevens)

The painting must resist the eye
almost successfully. Example:

The bird ruffling its wings resists
identity. The necklace it carries resists

our need for making sense—cranberries,
or pearls? And why the seductive unstringing?

Accept the beads, the lovely string curled
in one place only. And wingspots, too,

though they remind one of a butterfly.
Other butterflies migrate, this bird stays,

flirts. If a bird can lift a skirt hem,
showing her ankles, this is it.

A horror of birds that suddenly are real,
or not. We must endure our dreams all night,

the man leaning in a tree, poems dangling
on strings, his resemblance to your father,

until the obvious multicolored bird stands
motionless, no longer able to flutter, or sing.

Stowaway in the Arugula

A lighter green, almost yellow,
        than the notched leaves
                of the arugula, bound

in bunches and six bunches
        clumped together in a plastic bag.
                I glimpsed you among one,

folded like a tripod in the midst
        of that clump, stems of the plant
                like bars rising to cage

you in. Dead, I thought at first, before
        seeing half of one antenna
                wave and twitch. How warm

the kitchen must have felt after
        the fridge's tomb, then a rush
                of water, draining in the sink.

Oh small traveler, grasshopper hitching
        its ride, air freight from California,
                what could I do but wish

you well. As a West Coast transplant
        myself, I wanted to say good
                luck with months of coming dark.

Let it be enough that I held you
       in my palm for a few minutes,
              carrying you outside

like an elevated host, before
       setting you down (all of us go
              down), into green unknown.

Across Barbed Wire

Day when the clouds turn to buttermilk by 2 p.m.,
clouds churned thick and transformed to a yellowish-white,
and whatever twists you follow in country roads,
whatever meanderings take you from the main highway,
bring you to a gate, a house, a porch,
leave you at the white door in the garden, four brick walls,
      a spot to sit.

The horse noses pasture grass until you wave,
brown animal with blazed forehead crunching green
      until a hand lifts,
and the apple set out on the hand's table,
the red fruit offered on a palm,
becomes the call that beckons him,
changes into the invitation winding him
up the meadow's greening slope,
up the blazing hill.

It's mostly ridiculous how much we care,
both silly and not silly that it matters to us
who comes or sits, stays or talks,
who arrives or reclines, remains or speaks,
and yet it does—our muscles the storage places,
      hearts like attics

where dreams rise up on every side,
forests climbing inch by inch like green walls,
and hills show the scary expanses,
escarpments display all the frightening views
we thought we had left,
we hoped were gone.

No matter now.
It is not important today.
If you would not escape from me,
if you would not leave my side,
blazed horse or sweet man or kindly friend,
star-marked horse, man with eyes glittering,
        the friend who calls—

then let me say it,
then I'll pronounce it if you allow,
as the stars whirl around, a comet flares,
as galaxies wheel and a tailed ice-ball goes away
        for fifteen thousand years,
how much it helps me to feed you,
exactly what it means for me to nourish you
with my own outstretched paw,
my own extended, soft-palmed hand.

Once, Oval Beach

"You look at the sea
And search for its eyes

You look into eyes
And there see the sea." [from Carnac, by Guillevic]

i.
Large enough to be a sea
with swells, crisp waves

riptides depending on wind,
on-shore breezes, unpredictable water

Wading into it, deep, deeper,
then giving in to water

ii.
The seagulls, two, didn't fly
until one struggled, lifting off—

slowly, I stepped closer, breast-deep
in water—the gull's gold eye

suspicious, staring—then I saw
fishing line choking its neck, wings

iii.
Beak with a slight hook
it pecked my left hand—feathers white,

gray, black—with the other hand
I unwound, untangled—crooning

(where did the song come from?) oh gull,
calm now, winged one, let's get you free

iv.
A sense of grace lingered, a deep pleasure
to have helped aloft the one among us

meant to take wing above Lake Michigan waves

I was helper and intrepid one, not the caught
one, tangled and pinned on land.

New Year: The Lustrous Owl

1.
Astringent light, freezing rain.
The tax man ahead. The deep reckoning.

2.
Birds seen, books read, miles walked.
There's an app to keep track.

Why are owls so elusive? Heard,
but not seen.

3.
Sky drips water that coats pine needles.
Sticky as pitch. That front-yard fir,

the stuff golden like syrup on your hands.

4.
Birdbath filled with oak leaves.
A frozen stew.

5.
My sister picking at a blanket,
my sister's legs climbing the railing of the bed.

6.
Comparison is the thief of joy.

7.
The lustrous owl is not a species
but an artist rendition.

Black eyes, golden-tipped feathers.

8.
Eight in a row. A shooting gallery.
One goes down.

The county fair: chaos of sights, smells.
Cotton candy, grease of popcorn.

Ticket stub torn in half.

9.
I dreamed she was a skull on the floor.
The dog wanted to sniff—

no, I jerked the leash.
Jean was on her knees scrubbing,
scrubbing.

10.
Unwind the lights from the trees.

11.
In the front yard, swinging from the magnolia,
planetary balls—

my favorite: gold—

there is also crimson, citron.

12.
Snow tops them.
Ice will cause them to fall.

13.
Be prepared with an alternative heat source.

14.
A remote eye—we watched the end.
The same blanket

pulled up over her head.

15.
No other year but this, the one behind
not yet fading.

And this one? A dream swirling to shape.

16.
In another one, she called to me.
I stepped into a shallow boat—

And motion took us.

Acknowledgments

Thanks to the generous editors who welcomed my work into the pages of their journals.

Atticus Review: "Aerodynamic"
The Adirondack Review: "Air Like a Sea"
Black Market Review: "By Clear and Clear: Riverside, Mid-day"
Driftwood: "After Franz Marc's 'The Red Deer' (1912)"
Escape into Life: "Ghosts That Need Consoling" and "Wreath for the Red
   Admiral"
The Huffington Post: "Bird Carrying a Cranberry Necklace"
Imagination & Place: "Across Barbed Wire," and "Rockweed, Knotted
   Wrack, Dead Man's Fingers"
New England Review: "Ecclesiastical"
Plume: "New Year: The Lustrous Owl"
PMS (PoemMemoirStory): "Winter Nests"
Santa Clara Review: "The Prodigal Daughter"
Superstition Review: "Ravine Goddess, August"
Terrain.org: "Tent Caterpillars"
Unsplendid: "Occurrence with an Elephant Head"
Zone 3: "Homage to the Green Heron"
"Heron in Sunlight" and "Oscine" first appeared in *Sunday Rising* (Michigan
   State University Press, 2013).

CPSIA information can be obtained at www.ICGtesting.com
Printed in the USA
LVOW08s0501260816

501962LV00001B/49/P